What Can  I Read?

Adria F. Klein and Barbara Schubert

Illustrated by Sherry X. Chen

꩜ Dominie Press, Inc.

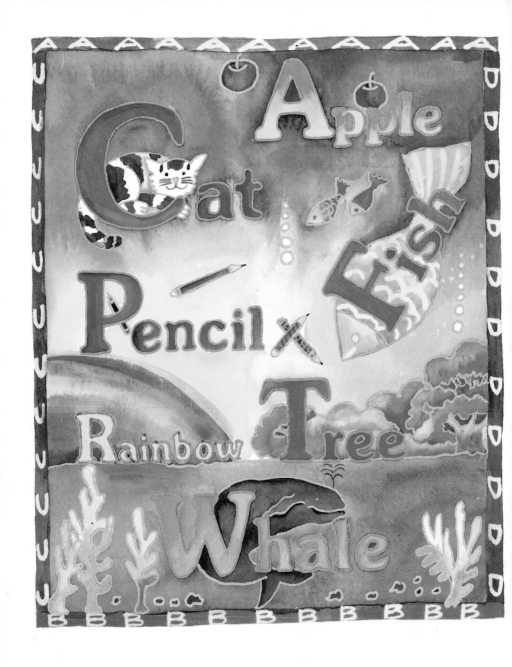

I can read words.

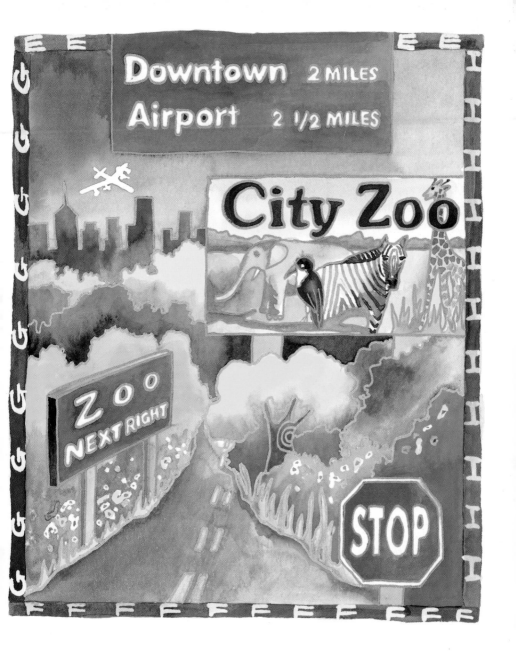

I can read signs.

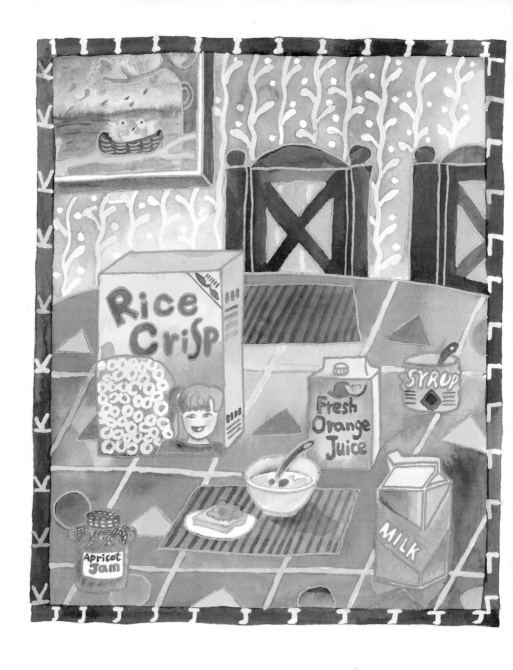

I can read labels.

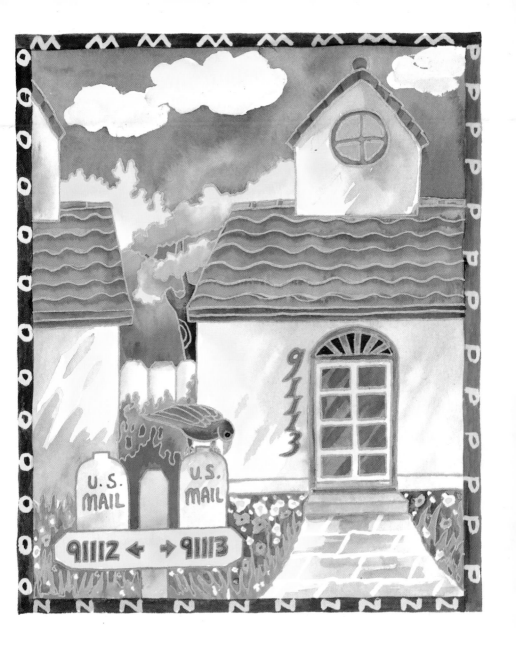

I can read numbers.

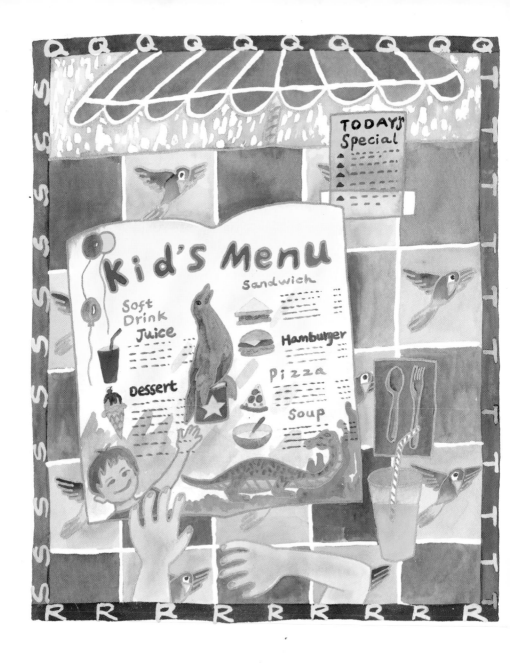

I can read menus.

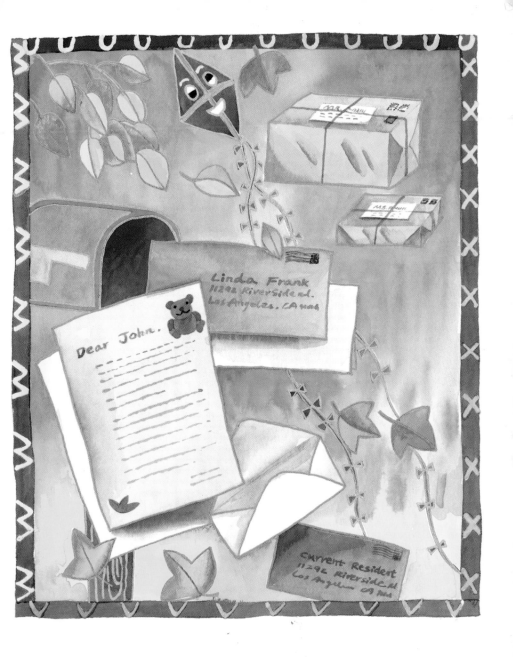

I can read letters.

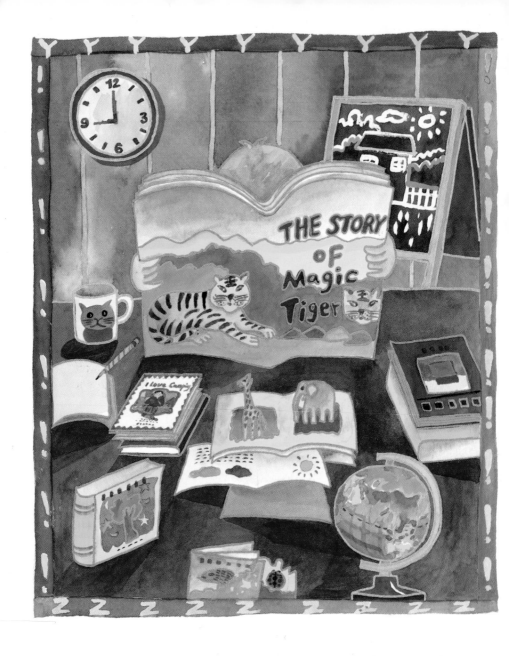

I can read books.